The Complete Guide to Internet Marketing for Marketing Professionals

You know the basics –Now Master the Trade

Authored by:

- **Khushi Priyanka**
- **Anurag Kartik**
- **Lalit Malhotra**
- **Binod Prasad**
- **Satish Das**
- **Sameer Ranjan**
- **Jyoti Jitendra Prasad**

About this Book:

We have been into Internet Marketing for past 19 years and have helped dozens of websites to go viral. The key websites being promoted by us are fommy.com, bluecellworld.com, bayt.com, flipkart.com, snapdeal.com, infibeam.com, pepperfry.com and many more. People come to know about your websites, when they search for some goods on internet, or they see your ad on internet. Then they do some shopping from your website and tell others to do shopping from it. Once they get customer satisfaction and cheap stuff, then they become your loyal customer. They shop repeatedly from your website, and keep on telling others about your website. Their belief is reinforced when they see newspaper advertisements and television ads about your website. Your website become popular and viral and your bank accounts keep swelling.

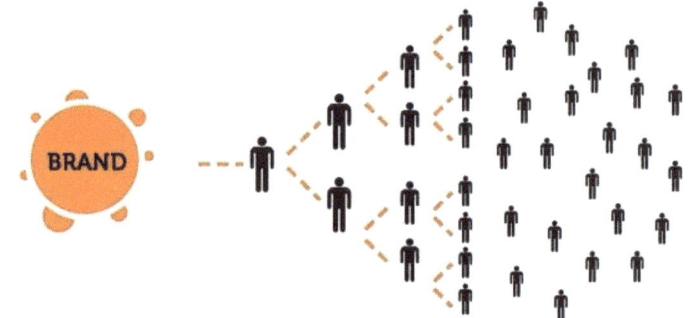

The Digital Version of Book is available at:
http://www.amazon.com/gp/product/B01CNAMA1Q?

Chapters

1. Having a Proper Website
2. Search Engine Optimization
3. Google AdWords
4. Twitter Marketing
5. Facebook Marketing
6. LinkedIn Marketing
7. Forum Posts, Posts in Jobsites
8. Banner ads in Traffic Exchange

9. Affiliate Marketing, Classified Ad sites

10. Army of Advertisers –Chain Email

11. Writing Ebooks

12. YouTube Marketing

13. PTC Sites

14. Final Word on Internet Marketing

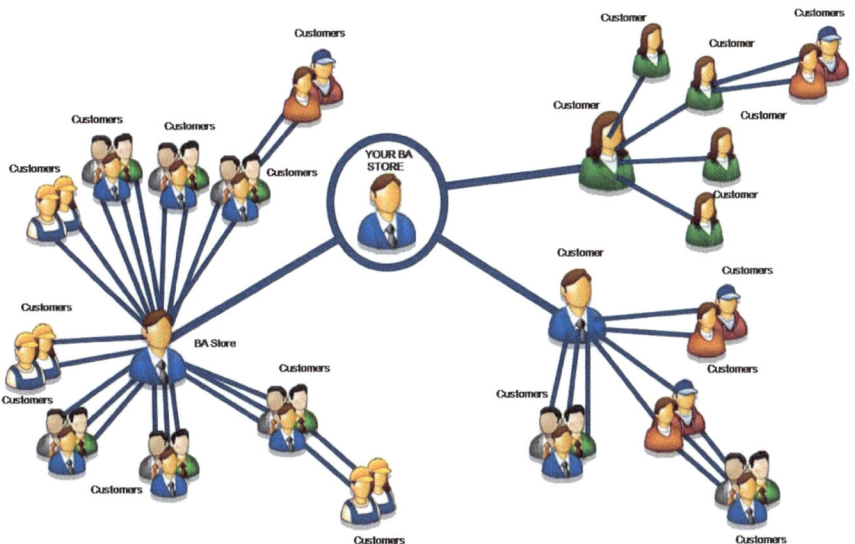

Chapter 1: Having a Proper Website

In IITs, when we were first introduced to Internet, then the first thing which we did was chatting. We thought that Internet was made only for chatting. We used to spend majority of time online with girls from Singapore, who also offered us to come to Singapore and attend Shahrukh Khan Concert for free.

In 2015 also majority of people at Facebook, plentyoffish, flirchi remain engaged in chatting only. So the basics are same, only interface has charged. And the only mistake you always do is to put your Credit Card Number in these kinds of sites.

Now I would like to ask you whether you would be interested in chatting on Linux interface as we did in 1996. Would you like to chat on Yahoo messenger as you did in 2009? The interface of interaction matters the most for us, and we would prefer a clean, attractive interface with lot of features.

Similar thing happens when a visitor visits your site. If your website looks poor; has dumb design and bad content then the user will definitely leave your site. According to a research a visitor takes decision in first 19 seconds whether to stay on your site or not. And if your site is not good with fancy interface then 88.33% of visitor will never visit your site again.

The first website I designed was the site of Naval Architecture department of IIT Kharagpur. The site was good but what I did was to put lot of photos with links to external websites. The system administrator of my department got mad at me and I never designed a site again at IIT as a professional.

But I am a freaky guy. I used to secretly design websites with lot of photographs and uploaded it at Tripod, Angelfire and Geocities. My friends used to say: "You are Mad". Yes I am mad. If you do Google search about my name then also you would find that I am mad. But I call myself "Crazy". That is a better word. I am very passionate about success. I never give up until I succeed.

As Steve Jobs said: "People who are crazy enough to think that they can change the world are the ones who change the world."

Next in 2001 I designed a site called kreativeinstinct.com the site was good in content but the only drawback was a swirling flash banner at the entry which read: Welcome to Kreative Instinct.

We designed many websites later, but the designs of websites were dumb and visitors said yuck while entering the site.

Coming back to kreativeinstinct.com my friends again yelled at me -You are Mad. Actually that site intended to be collection of short stories, and I gave my concept to themestream.com for free.

This time I took feedback from my friends seriously and stopped designing sites till 2005 and focused on my writing career. That time I thought that there is no site in India for real-estate and used vehicles, so why shouldn't I launch one. I launched gaadibangla.com and a consultancy site isolglobal.com. Both sites were designed in Microsoft FrontPage. They were pathetic in design but very rich in content.

Then I started being business minded. I thought I am investing $100 per year on websites but I am not getting any return. Is there any way I can monetize my sites. I also started thinking – Is there anyone looking at my sites or not? Then in 2005 I discovered statcounter.com and for past 10 years I had been a loyal customer of stat counter. In June 2005 I noticed that there are hardly any visitors to my websites and whatever hits I get is from the link mentioned in my email signature. I started exploring avenues to get more traffic. Then I stumbled upon Yahoo Groups. When I started posting in Yahoo Groups the traffic to my websites exploded. There were almost 300-400 visitors every day.

Visitors are important to your website, but also the look and feel of the site. You should go for free host like wix.com or wordpress.com only till you are amateur. But once you are launching a business, do not go for free hosting. Go for proper websites. The best hosts are hostgator and net4.in. Godaddy is good but arrogant. It can wipe your internet empire within seconds. If you want to contact me then fill the contact form of either of my websites kalkie.in, kalkie.org, igurucool.in, cidf.in

Now the next thing is web design. When you have so many beautiful templates available on internet then why you would do it yourself. Google "CSS3 template" or "HTML5 template" and you will get lot of beautiful templates on Internet. The editor which you should use for editing the template should be "Coffee Cup Html Editor"

First design your index page, put meta tags, title, Google analytics code and statcounter code in index page and then make multiple copies of your index page and hyperlink them. You can edit content later.

The file transfer protocol (FTP) client should be filezilla. There are plenty of tutorials in YouTube how to use filezilla. If you want to learn about html then also you can learn about it on YouTube. If you want to keep your email secret to your visitors then you can use foxyform in the contact section of your website. The messages from foxyform would be directly delivered to your inbox. If you want your website designed in PHP then you can get it done at www.upwork.com or www.guru.com

The Digital Version of Book is available at:
http://www.amazon.com/gp/product/B01CNAMA1Q?

Chapter 2: Search Engine Optimization

How would you like to have free traffic for your website? Suppose your website is on cab services and if someone searches cab services on Google and your website comes in first page, then your phone would start ringing at regular intervals. The key to rank higher in search engines is links and more the number of links to your website, higher your website would rank in search results.

I learnt SEO all by me and my site kalkie.in used to rank #3 for keyword VC funding. My expired site igurucool.com was #4 in Google for keyword online tutor. Some freaky guy put thousands of back links of these two sites on porn sites and my rankings disappeared. I can again rank my sites on top but I have no time. I am getting regular business through multiple sources and I would insist that you too should have multiple ways of attracting traffic to your website.

Well now I will teach you how a link looks like. Type:

<a href="http://www.kalkie.org"> Work from home, Online Jobs, VC Funding</a>

In your notepad and paste it at the bottom page of your index.html (Remember first page of your website is always named index.html)

When you open the index page in your browser and click on hyperlink you will come to my site and I gained a link and +1 vote to rank my site higher for the given keyword.

Keep that link on your front page and give me your link. I will place it on my site and tell others reading this book to do so. You will benefit because eventually our link will be put on so many sites.

Moving on!

As per Google standards there are two types of links Do follow and No follow. Do follow links count more and have 90% weightage in ranking your site whereas no follow links have 10% weightage in ranking your site.

But before you go for link building let me teach you how to optimize your webpages for search engines.

When you open the html of webpage then you can see a section called title. Suppose if you have to optimize your webpage for "cab services in New York" then put the title of your webpage as "cab services in New York"

Then just below the head section of html there is a section called meta tags. It is important for you to put your keywords in the meta section of the html. In "keywords" put "cab services in New York" and in description put "Good and affordable cab services in New York."

As far as the content of your webpage goes the phrase "cab services in New York" should be 3-4 times. Optimize all your pages like this. Suppose there is a page called "sight-seeing in New York" then ideally the name of page should be sight-seeing-in-new-york.html

Optimize all pages of your website like this. Al though you can also put alt tag for images, use <h1>, and other stuff too, but initially you have to build a brand and get these things done by professionals.

So this was about on-page optimization and now let us talks about off-page optimization that is building back links to your site at other sites.

The first step would be to generate huge number of worthless links for your website, a majority of which will die over a period time, but those who survive will give powerful votes for your website. It is like sperms. 40 Million of them are ejaculated, 1-6 survive, they give birth to babies. Ok I have heard that a lady gave birth to six kids; is there a higher count? Please update my knowledge.

What you should do is to go to fiverr.com and order the menu exactly as I give:

1 Scrape Box blast of 25,000 links

2 25,000 Forum Profile Back links

3 800 Social Book Marking

4 19000 wiki links

5 300 Edu and Gov links

All will cost you $28.

So you have generated 77,300 links a majority of which will be no follow links. Next search for directory submission and get your keywords and website submitted in 1000 directory for $25-$50. These 1000 links will be do follow links. You can check the spike in your link profile at www.majestic.com or www.ahrefs.com

After doing some destructive work, do some constructive work. And once you get some returns from constructive work then keep on doing only constructive work. Now create a link page on your website links.html and start exchanging links from sites like www.linkmarket.net and www.link2me.com. Register on site www.dropmylink.com and start building high value links on blogs, forums and edu or gov sites. Edu and Gov sites have high weightage in Google algorithm and you can attain high ranking with these links.

Devote one hour daily on link building for Lord Shiva, Maa Parvati, Bajrang Bali sake or any God you have faith in. Have you heard of Google Penguin; Google Panda or Google Humming Bird –they are nothing but algorithms developed by Google to rank your sites.

The sites are ranked on various factors. Let me elaborate these factors from Google's point of view:

- Domain Authority –The content in Wikipedia, LinkedIn and other top sites will have high ranking.
- Freshness of Content
- Number of do-follow backlinks
- Number of no-follow backlinks
- Social Signals from content posted in YouTube, Facebook, LinkedIn, SlideShare, Twitter etc.
- Keyword Density –The ideal keyword density in content should be 5-10%
- Meta Tags –So that Search Engines can crawl the keywords in Meta Tags.
- Relevance of Content
- No of Mentions in Social Media, Groups and Forums
- Page Rank – That is the quality of Backlinks
- Mobile Friendliness of Site –If your site is mobile friendly, ranking is higher.
- Age of the Site –Older the site, higher would be its ranking
- Popularity of the Site – Depending upon the Alexa Rank of Site, the keywords are ranked. (Suppose there are 1 million hits to your website within hour, and then all keywords would rank in top 10).
- Speed of the Site –The lesser time the site takes to load –higher it would be ranked.
- Security of the site –(https:// sites are ranked higher)

Now I elaborate the importance of Search Engine Ranking or Search Engine Optimization. Most companies need SEO. Below I have given the top 10 reasons elucidating that SEO is important:

- Online visibility improves conversions. Most of the people in India came to know about Flipkart, when they searched for a particular product and it was available on Flipkart.
- It generates leads. SEO is one of the best ways to generate leads. SEO is so great because it allows you to earn leads from a variety of different places and platforms online including YouTube, Flickr, Instagram and local search queries through Google, Bing, and Yahoo. In fact, SEO leads have a 29% close rate, while Social Media leads have 17%.

- You know about your competitors. When you search for a particular keyword, you would learn - who are your close competitors, and how you have to close ranks on them.
- SEO helps improve your visibility. By seeing your website, video, articles, posts and shares, people come to know about your products and would like to interact with you.
- SEO improves user experience of your site. By doing SEO your site has good navigation; website has relevant and unique content; website has no broken links or 404 errors. To get higher rankings you give your website an engaging design.
- SEO builds you brand reputation and credibility. By seeing your website in top of search results, people think that you are a good seminarian.
- It attracts the right people at the right time. Suppose someone is searching for old laptop, and your site surfaces at the top of results; then the visitor would be more interested to deal with you.
- It makes your site mobile friendly. To get good ranking, you have to make your website mobile friendly.
- SEO saves your advertising expense. SEO means free traffic for life. The money you might have spent on advertising is saved.
- SEO helps you to be a steady player. If there is constant flow of traffic to your website, even without generating much revenue, you would be steady with your biz.

Now coming to the meta tags, and title. Let me elaborate on them further in this section. I suppose you know the basic HTML, but for your convenience I am copying the lines of codes from my website:

```
<!DOCTYPE HTML>
<html>

<head>
  <title>Sunny -The Hot Religion,Shani Sanatan Dharam or Dharma. New
Religion Sunny, Venture Capital Funding, VC Funding Consultant, Work
from Home, Work at Home, Online Jobs, Home Tutor, Online Tutor</title>
  <meta name="End of Kaliyuga,Hot Religion Sunny, Shani Sanatan Dharam
or Dharma, venture capital funding, vc funding, vc funding consultant,
work from home, work at home, online jobs, physics tutor, chemistry
tutor, maths tutor, biology tutor, home tutor delhi, home tutor mumbai,
home tutor chennai, home tutor bangalore, online tutoring, home tutor
uk, home tutor usa, home tutor canada, online tutoring, work from home,
freelance jobs, Shani Deva, New Religion, Sunny the Hot Religion,
Jihad, Islamic Fundamentalism, Hindu Extremism, Hindu Fundamentalist,
Religious Intolerance" content="End of Kaliyuga, Shani Deva, New
Religion, Sunny the Hot Religion, Jihad, Islamic Fundamentalism, Hindu
Extremism, Hindu Fundamentalist, Religious Intolerance" />
  <meta name="End of Kaliyuga,venture capital funding, vc funding, vc
funding consultant, work from home, work at home. online jobs, physics
tutor, chemistry tutor, maths tutor, biology tutor, home tutor delhi,
home tutor mumbai, home tutor chennai, home tutor bangalore, online
tutoring, home tutor uk, home tutor usa, home tutor canada, online
tutoring, work from home, freelance jobs, Shani Deva, New Religion,
```

```
Sunny the Hot Religion, Jihad, Islamic Fundamentalism, Hindu Extremism,
Hindu Fundamentalist, Religious Intolerance" content="End of Kaliyuga,
Shani Deva, New Religion, Sunny the Hot Religion, Jihad, Islamic
Fundamentalism, Hindu Extremism, Hindu Fundamentalist, Religious
Intolerance" />
  <meta http-equiv="content-type" content="text/html; charset=UTF-8" />
  <link rel="stylesheet" type="text/css" href="css/style.css" />
  <meta name="fl-verify" content="3048afb38b49ec8ae92213fb9a9964e7">
  <!-- modernizr enables HTML5 elements and feature detects -->
  <script type="text/javascript" src="js/modernizr-
1.5.min.js"></script>
</head>

<body>
```

If you note that the title, Meta tags come between the opening and closing <head> </head> tag.
The appropriate title would help you to get indexed faster and higher rankings. The appropriate
keywords in Meta Tags and description would help you higher rankings for the given keywords,
and my strategy is to stuff as many keywords possible –as it is obvious from above. The text
written in the Meta tag would be shown in the search result.

Descriptions in the Meta tags tell audiences what they can expect to find on your page, and they
are persuaded those users to click. In a way, Meta descriptions are like Calls to Action.

These two images and the content above would give you a fair description of using Meta Tag.

If you have been typing in MS Word, then you would be aware of Heading 1 <H1>, Heading 2 <H2> and Heading 3 <H3>. The best strategy to rank your site higher with the search engines would be to write all keywords in all three fonts <H1>, <H2>, <H3> maintaining a high keyword density.

As far as images are concerned then use the <alt> tag to name the images in your website with a keyword. This will help image to be indexed by search engines, and by image search also someone might reach your website.

<h1>Heading</h1>

<h2>Heading</h2>

<h3>Heading</h3>

<h4>Heading</h4>

<h5>Heading</h5>

<h6>Heading</h6>

Now coming to nomenclature of inner pages of your website. This is the simplest part of the SEO, yet many people do not follow it. It is mandatory to get your website ranked higher in search engine, as well as your individual pages to be ranked higher in the search engines. Suppose your website has page about "cabs for rent in newyork", then the best thing to do is to name your page as: cabs-for-rent-in-newyork.html

You should change the title and the meta-tags of this page accordingly. The number of times the word "cabs for rent in newyork" should appear in the content should be between 4 and 8. Write logical paragraphs and emphasize on this phrase often.

Now if you put the above picture on the page of your website, then the best way would be to give alt tag of this image as "cabs for rent in newyork"

The syntax of a link is as following: <a href="http://www.igurucool.in">The Hot Religion </a>; the site is put inside the parenthesis and the keyword is put outside the brackets.
The best place to build backlinks is the Wordpress blogs and there are billions of them on the internet. They have three fields, and if you want to build links with them, this is the method

Name: Cabs for Rent in Newyork
Email: randy@newyorkcabbie.com
Website: http://www.newyorkcabbie.com

Comment: If you are in Newyork then please visit my website to have a nice ride around New York.

Do this to as many WordPress Blogs, Forums and Posts. The maximum number of times you link your keyword and website, the higher would be the search engine ranking of your website.

So this is the best method to increase your backlinks. The more number of WordPress blogs, where you leave a comment with your keywords and website reference, the higher would be ranking of your website. Now instead of using a long-tail name for the webpage, I use a simple page name called newyorkcab.html, for our website igurucool.in, and now I have to propagate http://www.igurucool.in/newyorkcab.html through-out the internet, just see what I am going to do.

The easy places to obtain high priority backlinks are Twitter, Facebook, Blogger, YouTube, LinkedIn and Google Plus. If you have started a new website and want 6000 backlinks then you can obtain 1000 backlinks each from these sites and it will also increase your social signals.

First with Twitter:
Tweet
#startup http://www.igurucool.in/newyorkcab.html
#crowdfunding http://www.igurucool.in/newyorkcab.html
@billgates http://www.igurucool.in/newyorkcab.html
@shanisadh19 http://www.igurucool.in/newyorkcab.html

Similarly in 40 groups of Facebook post the URL

In 1000 blogs of blogger post the URL

In 1000 videos of YouTube post the URL in the comment field.

In 50 Groups of LinkedIn post the URL 20 times, within a span of one month

Make 20 Videos on YouTube, and share it 1000 times in Google Plus circles making another 1000 links.

(If you want any further tips then please write to me at: shivshakti1949(at)outlook(dot)com)

Link exchange is another method to increase your site popularity. There are two great sites through which you can exchange links with thousands of users. These sites are:

- Link2me.com
- Linkmarket.net

You can also search the web for link partners.

Keyword density plays an important role in indexing of pages. Keyword density means number of times the particular keyword should appear in the given page. For 100 words, the ideal occurrence of keyword should be 4 to 6. Do not cramp the webpage with keywords. If you are going to take help of a freelancer then it is advised to use long-tail keywords.

Now coming to the tools and services that are important for Search Engine Optimization -I have outlined the various search engine tools and services, which would be helpful in finding the number of backlinks, building backlinks and other seo related stuff.

- Ahrefs.com –For checking the number of backlinks
- Majestic.com –For checking the number of backlinks
- Dropmylink.com –For building Do Follow Backlink
- XML Sitemap –This is essential part of SEO, this can be generated at: https://www.xml-sitemaps.com/
- Prchecker.info – This can be used to check the page rank of your website.
- You can sign up for Google Analytics and Webmaster Tools from Google Console.
- Given below in red is the robots.txt file in which you only change the name of site and copy-paste it as it is:
  User-Agent: *
  Disallow:
  Allow: /index.html
  Allow: /books.html
  Allow: /contact.html
  Allow: /videos.html
  Allow: /donate.html

  Sitemap: http://www.igurucool.in/sitemap.xml
- Fiverr.com –For Building Bulk Links
- Seoclerk.com –For Building Bulk Links

I am giving direct links to the services from where you can build bulk links:

- https://www.fiverr.com/uptotop/make-25000-blog-comments-with-scrapebox-get-huge-link-juice
- https://www.fiverr.com/seo_cloud/do-seo-backlinks-pyramid-good-youtube-facebook-quality-edu-high-pr-iinks
- https://www.fiverr.com/spookseo/create-800-social-bookmark-seo-backlinks-ping-in-24-hours
- https://www.fiverr.com/volarex/do-18000-contextual-backlinks-from-6000-wiki-pages-including-real-seo-edu-links
- https://www.fiverr.com/alex_rumer/provide-over-20000-live-seo-blog-comment-backlinks-improve-your-link-building

These services would cost you around $30, but your links would be flooded on the internet. You would shoot to top rankings of all search engines except Google.

Building good links or do-follow links is time consuming and tedious process. When I checked last time on flippa, I saw that there were more than 1.7 million sites listed for sale. The web business is down the dumps and 98% of site owners are generating zero revenue. This is because they are not getting any traffic to their site.

Building do-follow links are tedious, but if you want to build them use dropmylink.com, and leave comments as I have mentioned in previous chapter.

DROP MY LINK

Use mostly WordPress blogs to comments. I think that if WordPress is down, then entire SEO business will meet Doom's Day. Again I stress, that search-engine rankings of the sites depend upon the following factors:

- Domain Authority –The content in Wikipedia, LinkedIn and other top sites will have high ranking.
- Freshness of Content
- Number of do-follow backlinks
- Number of no-follow backlinks
- Social Signals from content posted in YouTube, Facebook, LinkedIn, SlideShare, Twitter etc.

- Keyword Density –The ideal keyword density in content should be 5-10%
- Meta Tags –So that Search Engines can crawl the keywords in Meta Tags.
- Relevance of Content
- No of Mentions in Social Media, Groups and Forums
- Page Rank – That is the quality of Backlinks
- Mobile Friendliness of Site –If your site is mobile friendly, ranking is higher.
- Age of the Site –Older the site, higher would be its ranking
- Popularity of the Site – Depending upon the Alexa Rank of Site, the keywords are ranked. (Suppose there are 1 million hits to your website within hour, and then all keywords would rank in top 10).
- Speed of the Site –The lesser time the site takes to load –higher it would be ranked.
- Security of the site –(https:// sites are ranked higher)

While you are building links, use Ahrefs.com to track your links –the screen shot from Ahrefs.com would look like following:

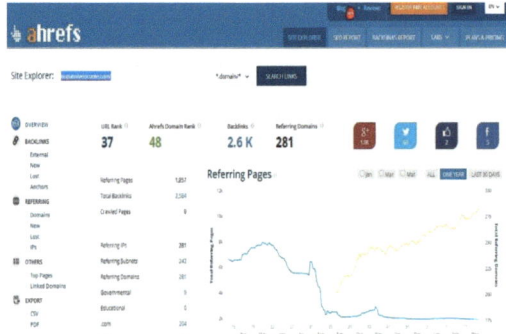

Here you get information about the following things:

- Total Number of Back Links
- Total Number of Referring Domains
- Total Number of EDU and Gov Links
- Social Signals

The importance of Edu and Gov Links is that it carries 20 times link juice more than a normal Do-follow Backlink. And as I mentioned earlier –more the number of referring domains to your website –higher will be the ranking of Website. So if you go for Bulk links, immediately 2500+ domains will start pointing towards your website.

Another handy tool to analyze your backlinks is majestic.com; here are few screen shots from the site:

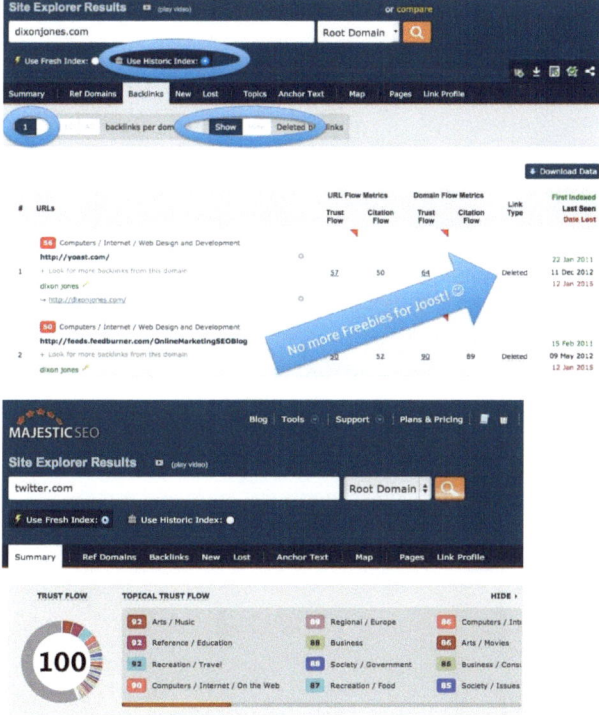

Count of TopicalTrustFlow_Topic_1

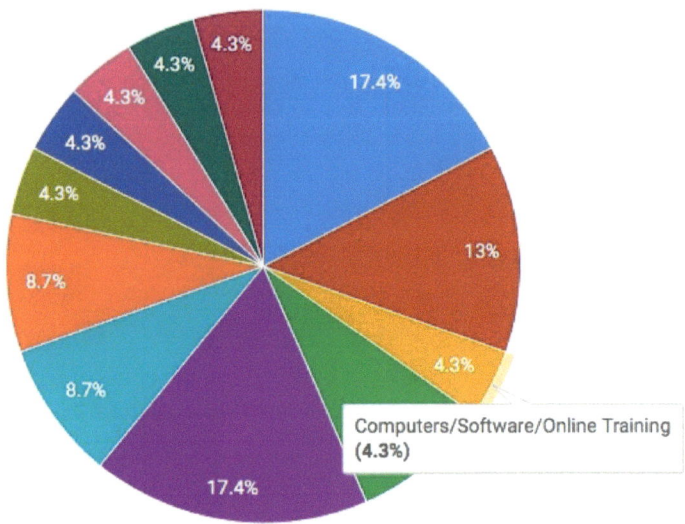

Computers/Software/Online Training
(4.3%)

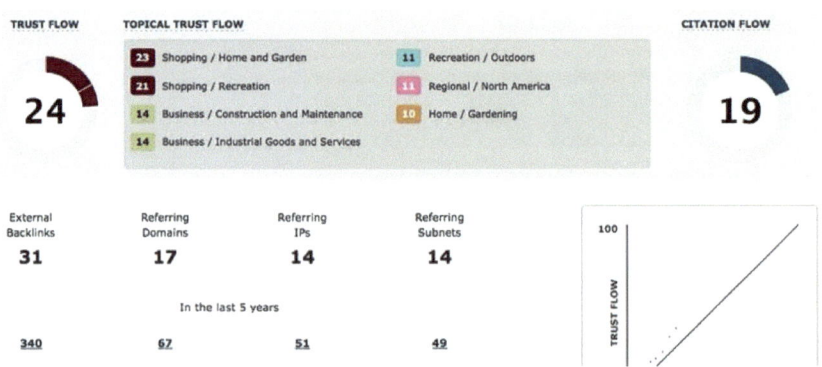

Use Analytics from Majestic.com to see the progress of your link-building efforts.

Now you would be able to find most of the edu or gov blogs with the help of Dropmylink.com, but in case you are unable to find, here is the strategy: In order to find edu and gov blogs, we have to use specific Google searches that give us .Edu or .Gov results for keywords we search. Paste the following searches into Google and put your main keyword into the "keyword" section of the code:

site:.edu inurl:blog "comment" -"you must be logged in" -"posting closed" -"comment closed" "keyword"

site:.edu "no comments" +blogroll -"posting closed" -"you must be logged in" -"comments are closed"

site:.gov "no comments" +blogroll -"posting closed" -"you must be logged in" -"comments are closed"

inurl:(edu|gov) "no comments" +blogroll -"posting closed" -"you must be logged in" -"comments are closed"

site:.edu inurl:wp-login.php +blog

site:.gov inurl:wp-login.php +blog

site:.edu inurl:"wp-admin" +login

By using these searches, you can locate blogs with .Edu or .Gov extensions, allowing you to gain extra link juice for your links.

Now to sum up, here are the top 21 things -which you have to keep in mind while doing SEO:

1. Commit yourself to the optimization. SEO is not a one-time event. SEO requires a long-term mindset and commitment from your side.

2. Have faith in your ability and remain patient. It takes months before actual results start pouring in.

3. If you are hiring a SEO company then ask questions about the tactics they are adopting to rank your site and time frame.

4. Learn SEO all by yourself. It is an art. More you practice, more perfect you will become.

5. Have analytics like ahrefs.com, majestic.com, statcounter.com and Google Analytics to measure your efforts.

6. Follow the rules of SEO to build an attractive website with sitemap and robots.txt in place.

7. Include a site map page. Spiders can't index pages that can't be crawled.

8. Make the navigation of your site simple.

9. Do keyword research at the start of web business? Use the free versions of Keyword Discovery or Word Tracker. Another good free tool is Google's Ad Words Keyword Tool.

10. Run a PPC campaign either in Google's Ad Words or Facebook, and measure results. This will keep you happy till SEO starts showing results.

11. Write a unique and relevant title and Meta description on every page.

12. Write for your users, not for the search engines. It's the users who buy, not search engines

13. Write great and unique content; keep it refreshing every now and then.

14. Use your keywords as anchor text when you are linking your webpages internally.

15. Do directory submission at trusted sources. One of the trusted sources for directory submission is Directory Maximizer (http://www.directorymaximizer.com). Do Dmoz and Yahoo submission as well.

16. Distribute Press Release wisely to gain media attention and create a niche for yourself.

17. Start a blog on Wordpress and link it to your site. Participate with other related blogs. Search engines, Google especially, love blogs for fresh content.

18. Use social media marketing to leverage your website. Make Facebook Fan-Page, Make Twitter account and link both buttons on front page of your website. Generate content for Quora and Yahoo answers, linking back to your website. Make more than 50K connections on LinkedIn and Post Regularly leaving links back to your website. You can use Flickr, Tumblr and Stumble Upon to redirect hoards of traffic to your website.

19. Make vantage point for local search opportunities. Ensure your site is listed in local/social directories such as CitySearch, Yelp, Local.com, etc., and encourage your visitors and customers to leave good reviews of your business on these sites, too.

20. Sign up for Google Webmaster Central, Bing Webmaster Tools and Yahoo Site Explorer to analyze how many numbers of links to your website are counted.

Chapter 3: Google AdWords

Many advertisers believe that giving ads in Google is the end of story. They would be flooded with sales and their bank account will swell; but this is not true. I knew of one advertiser from Mexico who wasted $10000 in Google AdWords and had zero sales. I also ran six campaigns in Google for Rs 3000 and had zero sales. During one of my interaction with AdWords representative in Hyderabad, the AdWords representative himself accepted that only renowned companies can generate sales through Google AdWords, but unknown products have negligible sales.

Now I shed some light on click through rate. Out of 2500 ad views in Google AdWords there is a single click –that too mostly due to curiosity.

You see lot of advertisements on Television but how many products do you actually buy? Same is true with advertisement on Internet. People see lots of products –but they seldom buy a product. It is very difficult to extract a penny from somebody on Internet.

The user will buy your product if he or she is engaged with you. Without engagement it is very difficult for you to sell something. Plus Google is whimsical. It keeps on suspending the accounts –and seasoned advertisers are reluctant to spend even a single penny on AdWords –because they fear that again Google will keep their money.

So do not advertise on Google unless you have a deep pocket. Google is good to create awareness, and it really needs a deep pocket to back up advertisements in Google. There is a huge competition for placements of ads and cost per click is very high. 98% of people will click your advertisement in Google just out of curiosity and never buy your product.

The most important thing is targeting. If you run your ads in Google, then target specific city, state or country. If you target worldwide audience –then most of the clicks would be from Africa, Pakistan, Bangladesh and Philippines and 70% of your money would be wasted. So always exclude these countries.

A majority of sales in Google AdWords come from USA, Canada and Europe. If you have global products then do remember to target these countries. A banner ad in Google is suggested because it has high visibility and people will not click on your Ads. The message is conveyed through banner itself.

The best way to advertise in Google is to go for banner advertisements. Your product will go viral and there would be good sales.

Now I tell you -how to run your advertisements in Google AdWords

Step 1: Signup for a Google AdWords Account

Visit Google AdWords and signup using your Gmail account. Signing up for AdWords is free; you pay only when you start running advertisements. It is likely that you would receive $100 or Rs 2000 AdWords credits. Fill up your name, address and contact number. It is likely that AdWords representative may contact you to help you running your ads.

Step 2: Determine what you want to advertise on Google, and who are your target audience?

You have to decide -what you want to advertise on Google and which category of people are your target audience. Suppose you want to advertise about Business Loan -then your target audience is small and medium sized entrepreneurs.

Step 3: Do Keyword Research

Keywords are the phrases that people search on Google. If you want your ads to be shown in Google search results, or on websites having similar keywords, then keywords are the phrases which trigger advertisements. Once you have decided them then login to your AdWords account, go to "Tools and Analysis" and click on "Keyword Tool". Type in the keyword that you think would attract customers, and then AdWords will display the estimate number of searches per month for that given keyword. If you click on the "keyword suggestions" tab at the top of displayed tab, it also gives you a list of related keywords which could attract traffic, and the estimated number of searches using those keywords.

Step 4: Starting Your Campaign

Click on the campaigns link from the top menu of AdWords console and then select create new campaign. Then you can set up a new campaign

Campaign Name: You can start with one campaign -but the method I use is of two campaigns- one text ad, another banner ad.

Campaign Type: The advertisements run on Google's search and display ad network by default. The results from display network are better because costs are low and there is higher visibility.

Locations: It is important to choose locations for the business. Never target African countries and countries like Pakistan and Bangladesh. If you are local business then choose within your city limits only.

Budget: Next you have to set your default bid-the maximum you can pay per click and maximum daily budget. I put default bid to $0.05, and maximum daily budget to $1. This way you can get 23-24 clicks, but there is no guarantee of sales.

Ad Extensions: The ad extensions allow for things like address, phone number, and Google plus Page for your business. It is better you do not include them. Keep your ads sweet and simple.

Step 5: Writing your ads.

Be creative in writing your ad. The best combination would be of something catchy and something which conveys the message.

The headline should hold the attention of user
Description line 1 should arouse users' interest in your product.
Description line 2 should develop the desire of user in your product.
And finally, the Display URL should reinforce a user's decision to take a determined action.
When user reaches your landing page then he should feel the urge to get the product.

Step 6: Make Your Campaign Live, Evaluate the metrics, and optimize the Results.

When your campaign becomes live, do not change the ad and keywords for one week. If you have installed Google Analytics in your website, then analyze which are the best performing keywords, and are you generating sales or not? Change the Keywords and Ad accordingly -so as to get maximum return for your investment.

Chapter 4: Twitter Marketing

Internet marketing has become very erratic; there is no fixed source from where you can get lead, traffic or revenue; so the best suggestion for you is to have multiple sales channels, multiple revenue streams – because to be frank –people on internet are unwilling to spend even a single penny on something new. Though the shopping sites are doing brisk business, but due to huge infrastructure they are supporting – they are also running in losses.

Twitter has evolved as a new medium for brisk Internet marketing and people are earning good money from their twitter marketing efforts. Suppose you tweet a product to 100K of your followers and 10 of them purchase the product, then you made cool $20 from your one tweet, assuming your profit from One product was $2. Twitter has personal interaction. If you tweet your product to one celebrity and they re-tweet you, then you can earn up to $2000 from a single endorsement by a celebrity.

There are other methods of Twitter Marketing too. You can advertise on Twitter to gain followers and keep on tweeting good products to them. As I said earlier –People are unwilling to spend a single penny on Internet, until they get something –they actually wanted. If you want to sell on Internet then sell only sub $10 products. No one is interested to buy anything –which is going to cost them $10 or above. Gone are the days when Gurus were selling $47 courses on Clickbank.

Now let us talk about an actual product –which costs you $5.99 –a perfume for valentine, then three days before Valentine's Day you start tweeting:
#Valentinesday Buy Good perfume from me: t.co/stxry
#StValentine Buy Good perfume from me: t.co/stxry
#Feb14 Buy cheap perfume from me: t.co/stxry

Suppose you are selling perfume for a charitable cause, then you can tweet:
@billgates –Buy perfume and help a charity t.co/stxry
@georgesoros –Buy perfume to help a poor t.co/stxry

But it is difficult to gain followers if you have a new Twitter Account. The best sites to gain followers are:
- Like4like.org
- Traffup.net
- Followlike.net

- 500followers.com
- Followersite.com
- Fastfollow.info

The Twitter marketing is the latest trend to make a product viral. If many people re-tweet your link then rush of buyers line up to buy your products.

Keep working in these sites until you gain a steady number of followers. Do not buy followers from cheap sites; otherwise your Twitter account will be blocked.

In some of the six sites, I mentioned above, there is a provision that you compose a new tweet on the site or copy the status from Twitter and after earning some points in these sites, you allow other people to re-tweet your tweets. This way your tweets will become viral. In Traffup.net, assign 50 points for re-tweeting your tweet and 10 points for liking your tweet. This way your tweets would be re-tweeted to thousands of people at zero cost.

In like4like.org and followlike.net you can embed your Twitter status with Tweet Id, and after you assign some points to the tweet, and then it would be re-tweeted to thousands of users automatically. In 500followers.com it is advisable to follow sponsored listings only. For every sponsor you follow, you gain five new followers. In your tweet, which would be re-tweeted it is important to put #hashtag, so that relevant people could be reached. For example

RT #valentinesday #stvalentines #Feb14 For the best perfume visit t.co/stxry.

Chapter 5: Facebook Marketing

The Alexa Rank of Facebook is 2. It is second most popular site in the world after google.com. It has more than 1.6 Billion users and it can help you get viral but only after YouTube and Twitter. The Alexa rank of YouTube is 3 and Alexa Rank of Twitter is 9. These three sites are the most popular social networking sites in the world. If you want your business to leave an impact then you should leave impact at these three sites. Advertising at social networking site is such a fun that you can enjoy at Orange Beach, Albama, USA and see visitors hitting your website. This is professed by some Internet Gurus that they are sitting at beaches and making millions. The million in this case is true –but only millions of hits to their websites, but a paltry amount of income. In real world it is very difficult to shell out a single penny from somebody, even from your father and mother; leave alone the visitors. Facebook is normally used by individuals for entertainment, fun, sharing videos and photographs; but you can use Facebook to generate leads for your business.

There are two ways through which you can generate leads –firstly by creating a post which would be seen by some of your connections and secondly by posting in big groups with lot of members – which could be seen by lot of people.

It would be much better if you create few groups of your own and start adding your friends from the list of friends in that group. Make it an open group so that everyone can post in that group. The secret groups and closed groups on Facebook are big distraction because everyone wants his/her voice heard. Pin your post at the top of your groups, and there would be a constant flow of traffic from the groups where you have pinned your post.

You should find those groups to join –which are in the line of your business. Suppose you are selling handicrafts then you have to find 40 groups related to handicrafts only. Join all the 40 groups and keep posting in them at a regular basis. If you post in these 40 groups daily, then definitely there would be 50-500 hits to your website directed from Facebook. There would be some sales.

The easiest method to find the relevant groups is to type in the search box of Facebook "Groups about Religion" or your own keyword. For example for my religion "Sunny" –I have six large groups related with Religion. I post in them at a regular basis.

I have created four groups at Facebook, and pinned my post at these groups. The pinned posts are giving steady flow of traffic to my products and website. Check out these four groups:

- Shiva Hanuman Kalkie Work from Home India America MLM
- Firangi Girlfriend Desi Friend
- Business Leads United States, India and Europe
- Dating Friendship Love Romance with Business

It is also recommended that you create a Facebook page about your product or cause, and gain likes by advertising on Facebook.

Do not forget to put Facebook like Button at the front page of your website. This will help you gain more loyal followers. Four things that are must on the front page of your website are:

- Facebook like page
- Twitter Follow Button
- Google Plus Button
- Add This Tool Box.

These four plugins will help you to get your website viral.

The Digital Version of Book is available at:

http://www.amazon.com/gp/product/B01CNAMA1Q?

Chapter 6: LinkedIn Marketing

LinkedIn is one of the top 10 sites in the World. Its Alexa rank is 10. It has 400 million members currently and its revenue is close to $ 2 Billion. It is used by sharp professionals, so if you have to promote a product like "Feng Shui" or "Work from Home" scheme it will not work in LinkedIn. The average income of members is over $100 K annually though there are some miser fellows asking for funding and there are scammers asking for $10000 upfront fees to arrange funding for them.

The best advantage of using LinkedIn is its spinoff SlideShare –which it recently acquired. If you make a PowerPoint presentation and upload it on SlideShare, then it would be seen by hundreds of people – plus the keywords which you have put in the title, description and tags of slides will come in the top of Google search results.

Now talking about LinkedIn Groups –the results were very effective till May 2015, but since then the groups have stopped yielding results. Earlier it happened that the most recent posts were at the top of groups; as many as 500 people read the post and 20-30 of them responded to the post. Earlier I used to do venture capital funding –sourcing clients from LinkedIn; but due to change in policy of LinkedIn –the funnel of clients dried up and I took other course for livelihood.

Now expecting that top slot for recent posts would be revived by LinkedIn –I give you the method –how to find groups, join them and post in them. To join groups let me concentrate on my earlier business – venture capital funding, business loan, working capital and private equity. Now follow these steps:

- Find groups about business loan in the search bar of LinkedIn
- A list of groups will come
- Join those groups which have more than 10000 members
- Wait for moderator to approve your membership
- Once your membership is approved, you can start posting in these groups about your products and services.

The leads from the groups were very effective earlier, but now no response comes from posts in groups. Let us see what happens in future.

Now there are only three methods left, through which you can get leads from LinkedIn. These are:

- Increase your LinkedIn connections daily and share updates with them. The more you share, more people will come to know about your product and services.
- Create posts about your products and services in LinkedIn and share it repeatedly in Facebook and Twitter. This will help you create permalink and your posts might come at the top of Google search results.
- Whenever you make a YouTube video, then besides sharing it on Facebook, Twitter, Google Plus –share it with LinkedIn Groups as well –who knows you might get leads from there as well.

The Digital Version of Book is available at:

http://www.amazon.com/gp/product/B01CNAMA1Q?

Chapter 7: Forum Posts, Post in Job Sites

There a quite a few forums from which you can get traffic, if you leave posts in these forums sending links back to your site. These forums are:

- Digital Point
- Site Point
- LinkedIn Posts
- Warrior Forum

- Emoneyspace
- Neobux Forum
- Clixsense Forum

Keep posting in these forums regularly and get 100-200 hits to your website daily.

Chapter 8: Banner Ads in Traffic Exchange

The ads in traffic exchanges is very effective to attract traffic. You can get loads of traffic from autosurf at www.hitleap.com. You can make banners in bannerfans.com and place it on bannerexchange.com, hit4hit.org and easyhits4u.com to get referral traffic.

Chapter 9: Affiliate Marketing, Classified Ad Sites

The affiliate marketing can be done with the help of shareasale.com, where you pay a commission to your affiliate, either for bringing traffic to your site or for a sale at your site.

Chapter 10: Army of Advertisers –Chain Email

Does email marketing works? Yes it works, it rocks? But the real problem is how you will get the email list. Google will not allow any ad with splash page and if you advertise in Facebook –it will be very expensive and very few people will opt to push their names in your email list. An Australian client of mine tried this on Facebook –he spent $100 on advertising and could capture only 3 emails. So what is the option? If you buy email lists from Internet it is worthless, because the click through ratio is very poor. Out of 3 million people whom you send the email –only 7-10 would click at the link given in the email. And more than 100 people were already bombarding them promotional emails after purchasing the list.
One of the options is to go for SEO of your site and collect all emails in your guest-book or in a pop-up window of your front-page. Normally major websites harness the emails in this manner.

You can learn SEO by book written by one of our expert. It is very handy and practical and this book means business. Most of the books on SEO are full with technical jargons and have very less practical information in them.

- The Ultimate Guide on Search Engine Optimization for Internet Professionals: The Bible of SEO
http://www.amazon.com/gp/product/B01CAJ1AGQ

SEO is one of the best methods to gather email list. The traffic which will come to your site will be naturally inclined in your product. Purchasing email list is the worst option, and you have to build your email list right from the scratch. This can be done by organizing a contest on your website. Have a dedicated page on your website which hosts contests and through Bulk SMS services tell the people to enter contest.

You can also tell the people to enter contests through Whatsapp groups, Facebook groups, Twitter and LinkedIn Groups. Once you gather an email list then send newsletter to all those people who have entered contest –once a week, and every week organize some contest. This is one of the best methods to make your website viral. If people get something from you –they will visit your site again and again.

Make some attractive posters in your cities and stick them at places from where you can get target audience. The best places to stick posters would be notice boards of society flats, libraries, bus stops, hotels, restaurants, schools and colleges.

Make pamphlets of your product and distribute it along with newspapers at minimal cost. You can also put classified advertisement of your product at leading classified sites of your country to attract traffic.

Chapter 11: Writing eBooks

You should write twenty eBooks about your product for length of thirty to forty pages and publish it online to increase the awareness about your website or product. Once people read your eBooks and if they find something interesting they would definitely visit your website to find something more about your product. Use Foxy Form to contact the visitors from your website, because if you give them your direct email they will spam you.

Collect data about your potential customers in an excel sheet and regular keep sending newsletters to them. The eBook is best written in Microsoft word and you do not have to go to any online editor as Microsoft Word itself checks for spelling mistakes and grammar. You can use freepdfconvert.com to convert your book into PDF format and distribute it through emails to your friends and associates. Do not forget to insert links about your websites in that book. Writing books can be additional source of income to you.

Chapter 12: YouTube Marketing

The social media plays an important role in Internet Marketing. The major social media channels are: Twitter, YouTube, Facebook, LinkedIn and Google Plus. You have to use them at fullest extent to generate leads and sales and to make your website viral. The best website for displaying and sharing video about your product or service is YouTube. If you ask how to make a video then it is pretty simple.

Make a Power Point Presentation in Microsoft Office and put information about your product and services in between of something informative. To see how product related video should be visit www.igurucool.in. Once you are done with Power Point Presentation, save the file and upload it to slideshare.net. After that in Power Point go to File > Save and Send > Videos > HD and Internet and save the video as .wmv file. The Power Point does it automatically. Set the spacing between each slides as 11 seconds in the video. If you put shorter duration then the viewers would not be able to comprehend the message conveyed in the video. After you upload your Video on YouTube – Make sure that you put keyword rich title, description and tags. Your video can be discovered by viewers only through the keyword –On Google or on YouTube.

Keep sharing your video through Twitter, LinkedIn, Posting video link in the comment section of YouTube, Facebook and Google Plus. More you share the video, more people will view the video and more people will come to know about your product and services. Never put a link in the description section of the YouTube or you would be banned from the YouTube, but it is ok to put your links in the comment section of other people videos. Once the video is published, be sure to review it and like it.

The best way of viral marketing is to keep on posting comments in the YouTube videos of other people. I just posted the following comment in the videos and within minutes I had 107 hits to my website.

Marry ten times, run fast cars, but bow to Sunny to go to Heaven:
http://www.amazon.com/gp/product/B01BION45O

www.igurucool.in

www.kalkie.in

www.kalkie.org

www.cidf.in

Jesus was not prosecuted on Cross. The Commander-in-chief of God's Army took Jesus to heaven, changed the face of king and hung him on cross. While putting bullets in shape of nails Kartikeya said Whatsapp.

Chapter 13: PTC Sites

PTC sites are getting paid to sites, where you get paid for viewing advertisements. There are only two genuine PTC sites –Neobux.com and Clixsense.com, rest all PTC sites are scams and are not stable. Neobux and Clixsense are active for more than 6 years and have paid over $10 million to their users. You can join these two PTC sites at www.igurucool.in/earn.html

The normal rates of advertisement at these two sites are $5 for 2500 visits to your website or clicks. These two sites are great for recruiting affiliate marketers. You should organize an affiliate page on your website and recruit people from these two websites and offer them 50% commission per sale they bring to you.

Chapter 14: Final Word on Marketing

At the end of your marketing effort different sources of traffic should point towards your site. This will happen when:

- If you have 3-4 inter-linked sites
- The job postings point towards your sites
- The slide share presentations point towards your sites
- The post in Facebook groups points towards your sites
- The tweets point towards your sites
- The banner advertisements point towards your sites
- The readers of eBooks visit your sites
- The listener of podcasts visit your site
- There are frequent visitors to your website through LinkedIn groups
- The viewers of YouTube Videos visit your site.

Your strategy should be to distribute traffic sources in such a way that traffic sources fire intermittently like snipers zeroing to their targets.

End of Book. Amen!

www.ingramcontent.com/pod-product-compliance
Lightning Source LLC
Chambersburg PA
CBHW041613180526
45159CB00002BC/829